IMAGES OF ENGLAND

# Walberswick to Felixstowe

IMAGES OF ENGLAND

# Walberswick to Felixstowe

Humphrey Phelps

First published 1994
This new pocket edition 2006
Images unchanged from first edition

Nonsuch Publishing Limited
The Mill, Brimscombe Port,
Stroud, Gloucestershire, GL5 2QG
www.nonsuch-publishing.com

Nonsuch Publishing is an imprint of Tempus Publishing Group



British Library Cataloguing in Publication Data.
A catalogue record for this book is available from the British Library.

ISBN 1-84588-329-2

Typesetting and origination by Nonsuch Publishing Limited
Printed in Great Britain by Oaklands Book Services Limited

# Contents


Introduction 7

1 Walberswick, Blythburgh, Dunwich 9

2 Westleton, Theberton, Sizewell, Leiston 35

3 Aldringham, Thorpeness, Friston, Knodishall, Snape 45

4 Aldeburgh 55

5 Orford, Hollesley, Alderton, Bawdsey 79

6 Felixstowe 87

7 People and Occasions 105

Picture Credits 128

1502. EAST CLIFFS. FELIXSTOWE. – JUDGES'

# Introduction

The photographs in this collection span a period of almost seventy years, from the last years of the nineteenth century to the middle of the twentieth. Occasionally some of them give the impression that the span is several centuries instead of seventy years. Many of the photographs were taken during the early years of the twentieth century, and some of the scenes they record are still just within living memory. Historically, not so very long ago; but looking at them we realise that it was long ago, far longer ago than the dates would have us believe. These photographs depict a different way of life, a different world ...

The motor car was still a novelty. Fishing was the dominant influence – even landworkers went fishing during the autumn and winter months and were known as 'half and halfers'. Beaches were alive with fishermen, boats and nets. Fishermen and their families were living in the fishermen's cottages, just as farmworkers populated the inland villages. Lifeboatmen braved turbulent seas and raging storms in boats powered by oars. The railways were bringing more visitors to Aldeburgh and Felixstowe, which had become popular resorts, and large hotels were being built to accommodate them. Felixstowe, said a London newspaper, 'basks in the sunshine of fashion'. On their beaches stood rows of those quaint contraptions called bathing machines, although why what were in effect huts on wheels were called machines is a mystery to me. Walberswick had become a powerful attraction to artists, the last of the old churches at Dunwich was tumbling into the sea. Leiston was a busy industrial town, with no pretensions to beauty but with a great reputation for the machinery manufactured at the Richard Garrett Works. Thorpeness was being transformed from a quiet fishing village to the fantastic creation of an 'olde worlde village' by G. Stuart Ogilvie. Trains running on the charming little Southwold Railway were still stopping at the stations at Blythburgh and Walberswick. Around Felixstowe, on farms now covered by concrete, men and horses ploughed land reputed to grow the best bread wheat in all England.

The muscle of men and horses was still the major source of power on the land – tractors did not appear in Suffolk until the First World War and did not become the major source of power until the Second World War. When the earliest of these photographs were taken corn was still harvested by gangs of men with scythes and hooks and crooks, as it had been for generation upon generation. The sails of windmills turned and the mills ground corn for man and beast. The blacksmiths were busy at their forges, the carpenters at their benches, the wheelwrights in their shops; the cobblers, the tailors and a host of other craftsmen and craftswomen were all engaged in supplying the needs of their parishes. A quiet but busy landscape, a landscape with figures; one which William Cobbett (who spoke well of Suffolk), Robert Bloomfield and Arthur Young (both Suffolk men, one a poet, the other first secretary to the Board of Agriculture), would have recognised. Even Thomas Tusser (the author of *Five Hundred Points of Husbandry*), who lived in Suffolk during the sixteenth century, would not have found the landscape depicted here as strange as it is to us today.

Even in the late 1940s men and horses could still be seen working in the fields, sheaves of corn in shocks still stood in the fields at harvest time. But when the latest of these photographs were taken the combine harvester was replacing men, horses and binders that cut and bound the sheaves, transforming a harvest scene that had endured for centuries. And not just the old harvest scene, as more machines came, ever bigger and more sophisticated, creating a different way of life, a landscape without figures: the age-old rural structure was destroyed.

With the decline in fishing a similar fate has descended on the towns and fishing villages, although I believe Aldeburgh has retained much of its character both in the town and on the beach where there are still several fishing boats and fishermen to be seen. Also the lifeboat, albeit a very different one to any seen in this book, is poised for action and still has a valiant crew composed of men prepared to risk their lives to save the lives of others.

Most of the photographs present these seventy years as an idyllic period but there was a harsher, darker side that should not be forgotten. Many people suffered hardships and poverty; some of those picturesque cottages were no more than damp hovels inside. Then there was the fear of the workhouse casting its shadow over many lives, a fear that persisted well into the twentieth century. Neither should we forget the people who were part of these scenes, especially those men clad in oilskins, or corduroys and hob-nailed boots, and their womenfolk struggling to feed and clothe families on a few shillings a week without all the amenities now regarded as necessities. The skill and endurance of these ordinary people on land or sea commands our admiration and our respect. As Doreen Wallace, the author of several Suffolk novels said, these people 'can teach us endurance, and skill in labour, and folklore, and humour, which is so much kinder than wit, and faith and hope and charity – in fact, everything about how to live on thirty bob a week and keep decent.'

The best of days, the worst of days, but what a pity that while getting rid of the worst in those days we also lost the best.

During all these years, before them and after them, the hungry sea has been devouring the land along this coast. Yet the coast itself remains and so does that immensity of light which can only be seen in this part of England. In a companion volume, *Lowestoft to Southwold*, I quoted from Julian Tennyson's book *Suffolk Scene*, published in 1939. He said that the real glory of Suffolk was its coast, and that its coast, by its very nature, was its saviour. It has kept the hand of man at bay. That is as true today as it was when it was written, except for a folly, which may yet prove the most expensive and dangerous of all man's follies. How much wiser were the makers of windmills who harnessed the wind.

The photographs are arranged as a kind of journey from the bank of the Blyth river at Walberswick to the sea at Felixstowe. As you cannot travel along the coast continually, this photographic journey, like the journey by road, is a series of detours, stopping at some inland places on the way. Lastly, there is a section on people.

I have made no attempt to place these pictures in chronological order. Neither have I attempted to make any comprehensive cover of any place or any subject. My aim has been less ambitious and all this book claims to do is to show glimpses of a period not so long ago but which now seems long ago. If it provides as much interest to the reader as it did to me in compiling it, I shall be well pleased. Although I must add, that for me it has been a bitter-sweet experience. I just cannot help thinking that too much of value has been cast aside, unnecessarily and thoughtlessly, in this process we call progress.

Once again, I have had valuable assistance from Suffolk friends, namely: Philip Kett of Walberswick, David Moyse of Reydon, Derrick Neave of Saxmundham, Jack Smith of Aldeburgh, John Tooke of Southwold and Bob Wright of Knodishall. To these and to Mrs Foss and the Aldeburgh Museum I tender my sincere thanks. Without them I could not have compiled this book – I can only hope that it meets with their approval and the approval of all those who love this delightful part of Suffolk.

Humphrey Phelps

*One*

# Walberswick, Blythburgh, Dunwich

'Swoul and Dunwich and Walberswick
All go in at one lousy creek.'

*Anon.*

The River Blyth at Walberswick. The Blyth once flowed into the sea near Dunwich until the channel, which now separates Walberswick from Southwold, was cut in 1590. The river, which rises near Laxfield, used to be navigable as far upstream as Halesworth.

*Above*: Blackshore, Southwold, looking towards Walberswick. The scene of some distress, possibly flood, *c.* 1900.

A fisherman on the River Blyth at Walberswick. William Addison described Walberswick as 'A decayed port with an air of mystery about it from its smuggling and privateering past that is now a favourite resort of artists.' In the fourteenth century the port supplied five ships to the Crown for the Navy. In 1451, it had thirteen barques trading to Iceland, Ferro and the North Seas, more ships than any other east coast port, and twenty-two fishing boats employed off this coast. Walberswick suffered greatly from fire. In 1633 a great part of it was burned. Fire struck again in 1683, and in 1749 one third of the remains were destroyed. But by 1840 it had a quay for vessels weighing up to one hundred tons. In 1619 a national subscription was raised to relieve people of Dunwich, Southwold and Walberswick whose misfortunes were, in part, blamed on pirates.

*Opposite below*: Walberswick Quay before 1900. The black hut in the centre was called the 'Savoy'; next to it is a smokehouse and on the left are artists' studios. All except the Savoy were lost in the flood. Note the wooden smacks. The letters LT denote that the vessels were registered at Lowestoft. Walberswick Church can just be seen in the background.

Walberswick Creek. In the nineteenth century, parishioners used to graze large numbers of geese on the Salt Marsh.

Walberswick from Southwold, c. 1920s.

The Ferry. Early ferry rights were invested in the Crown. Walberswick had one of the oldest ferries in East Anglia. The River Blyth Ferry Co. Ltd operated the ferry from 1885 to 1942. It is now a rowing boat ferry again.

The Ferry, looking from Southwold towards Walberswick. The Southwold and Walberswick rowing boat ferry was replaced in 1885 by a hand-cranked chain ferry, and later by steam power.

Walberswick.
'I always did love Walberswick and have in olden time,
Immortalised its lonely shores in sentimental rhyme.
Artists sketch the ferry hut, the reeds that sway and nod ... *(Punch)*.

Bell Hotel, Walberswick. At first glance the Bell Hotel looks the same as it does today, but in this picture it has a thatched roof which was burned in April 1949. In 1767, the bell of St Andrew's Church was sent to London by sea, and was re-cast at a Whitechapel foundry. On its return it was landed at the Quay, and in May 1768 it was rehung and five quarts of beer were supplied to celebrate the occasion at a cost of one shilling and threepence. The dreaded apparition Black Shuck, a hound as big as a calf with a coat as black as ebony and eyes that burn like live coals which is reputed to haunt Walberswick Green, has been seen between the Bell and the vicarage. The vicarage was destroyed by a bomb during the Second World War.

*Opposite below:* The original Kissing Bridge at Walberswick. This bridge was replaced by another which was removed during the Second World War and stored away. It was later found and used for firewood by the troops stationed at Walberswick.

High Street, Walberwick. In September 1918 Walberswick was the first village in East Suffolk to form a Women's Institute.

The Street, Walberswick. By the end of the nineteenth century there was a thriving colony of artists at Walberswick. Philip Wilson Steer, the best known, first came in 1884 and made regular visits until 1891. Other artists attracted to Walberswick were Charles Rennie Mackintosh and Francis Newberry.

*Above*: Ferry Knoll, Walberswick, *c.* 1910.

Walberswick, showing the sign of the old Anchor Inn on the left. 'The cottages seem to have been built and grouped together for the benefit of artists; the wooden bridges that span the dykes in the salt marshes are wonders of rustic work; the shanties in which the fishermen store their gear and smoke their sprats and herrings are delightful to the eye of the painter and a shock to the nerves of the architect; hulks, captsans, anchors, chains, spars, and every kind of wreckage lie strewn about in picturesque disorder; while ocean, river, salt marsh, heathland, firs, and the grand old ruined church, combine to make Walberswick a delightful little village and an ideal place for a quiet holiday.' (W.A. Dutt, 1909).

*Opposite below*: The Old Anchor Inn, Walberswick, Known in the 1840s, and for some time after that, as the Blue Anchor. In the 1920s the Anchor was pulled down and re-erected further up the street. It is now a private house known as Anchor Lea. A new building, also called the Anchor, which opened in 1929, was erected on almost the same site as the old Anchor. However, its old stables remain.

*Above*: The Mill, Walberswick.

A mine on Walberswick Beach, First World War. During the First World War there was an Army Training Camp on the Marshes. During the Second World War, Westwood Marshes were deliberately flooded as an obstacle to invasion and scaffolding poles were erected all along the beach.

*Opposite below:* The Mill, Walberswick, with the church in the background. The white building on the right is the Anchor. Its sign, which can just be seen, was later moved up the street and on the opposite side of the road.

The Street, Walberswick, *c.* 1935.

*Opposite below*: Walberswick Railway Station, 1902, the year in which the telephone was installed – note the pole by the waiting room. A larger station, complete with booking office, was built soon afterwards. Originally there was only one intermediate station, at Wenhaston. The Walberswick station was opened on 2 September 1881.

Walberswick Railway Station, early 1890s. Walberswick was situated on the Southwold to Halesworth line, which was opened on 24 September 1879 and lasted for fifty years. Note the fish boxes beyond the waiting room and the old swing bridge in the background. This station was adjacent to Walberswick Common.

The Southwold Railway near Blythburgh. The Blythburgh station was opened three months after the line had been in operation.

Southwold Railway Station. These are the passengers for the final journey, 11 April 1929, and the line closed completely soon afterwards.

Blythburgh. Washing on the line, a man with a horse and cart and, rather surprisingly, a lamp post by the corner of the churchyard.

Church Lane, Blythburgh. In Saxon times Blythburgh supplied 10,000 herrings to the Crown – the Monarchy, not an inn.

Holy Trinity, Blythburgh. The church took eighty years to build. Like the church at Southwold it has a Jack-o'the-clock, a wooden figure in medieval armour. At a Sunday service in 1577, a great storm struck the church which 'cleft the door, and returning to the steeple, rent the timber, broke the chimes ...' The steeple crashed through the roof and killed two members of the congregation. Scorch marks can still be seen on the door. Black Shuck's claw marks can also be seen. The church-wrecker Dowsing's men also played havoc in the church.

The Heronry, Blythburgh. The Southwold Railway ran along here. It was formerly known as Dead Man's Gully, and horses being ridden along here are said to behave in a strange, frightened manner although their riders see and hear nothing untoward.

London Road, Blythburgh (the A12). Note the motor cycle and sidecar in the foreground and the White Hart pub on the left.

Priory Road, Blythburgh. It is reputed that stealthy footsteps have been heard in the Priory.

WHITE HART INN

Toby's Barn, Blythburgh (destroyed in the 1987 hurricane). It stood on the opposite side of the Walberswick road to Toby's Walks. In 1750 Ann Blackmore, an attractive woman of Walberswick, was found dead near Blythburgh four-cross-ways. A black man, Tobias Gill, or Black Toby, a drummer in the local company of Dragoons, lay in a drunken stupor beside her. He was arrested and later found guilty of murdering the woman. Until the very last he protested that he was not guilty. On 14 September 1750 he was hanged on the spot known as Toby's Walk. Since then his ghost has haunted the crossroads, recklessly driving a hearse drawn by four headless horses.

*Opposite above*: Blythburgh White Hart, at one time an Ecclesiastical Court House.

*Opposite below*: Blythburgh White Hart, *c.* 1950. Ernest Reed Cooper, the author of numerous Suffolk tales, was born at Blythburgh in 1865.

The Splash, Dunwich. By this time only a small village, but Dunwich used to be a large town with several churches until it was washed away by what used to be called the German Ocean.

High Street, Dunwich. The post in the centre is the barrel of an old cannon, placed here to prevent parking on the Green. Two little girls in white, on the right, are posing for the camera. On the left is the Barnes Arms, formerly the Ship and now the Ship again.

High Street, Dunwich. The Barnes Arms (or Ship) has a flag pole – does the cannon also have a flag pole? The two women appear to be having a quiet chat.

The Street, Dunwich. Dunwich was once the capital of East Anglia and the see of a Bishop. It held a considerable position among the commercial cities of the kingdom.

The remains of All Saints Church, Dunwich, 1905. This was the last of the old churches of Dunwich and the last service held here was during the mid-eighteenth century.

All Saints Church, 1912. By 1919 all of the church had fallen into the sea.

The cliff and beach at Dunwich.
'There is a glorious City in the Sea,
The sea is in the broad, the narrow streets,
Ebbing and flowing ...' (Samuel Rogers).

The Round House at Dunwich. From 1914 to 1918 it was used as a guardroom by some of the Welsh Horse then stationed at Dunwich. Three troopers, shut within one night, declared they had seen the ghost of someone exercising an Arab mare and they described in accurate detail Miles Barne, who had been dead for a number of years and whom the troops could never have seen.

Dunwich children, early 1900s. The school building belonged to the Dunwich Estate and was sold in 1947 for £510. The school closed in 1964. Edward Fitzgerald, Thomas Carlyle, Jerome K. Jerome and Henry James all stayed at Dunwich.

*Two*

# Westleton, Theberton, Sizewell, Leiston

'There are places that are lovely
to visit because they are hard
to reach.'

*Norman Scarfe.*

The Green, Westleton, *c.* 1905, formerly called Westleton Common. The tall building on the left is the White Horse, which was rebuilt in 1898. In the centre is the Town Well.

The Mill, Westleton, 1908, a post mill with a round house. It is a particularly good view of the fantail which turned the buck (the body) so that the sails faced the wind. In the nineteenth century, Westleton had three windmills.

The Westleton Crown in the early 1900s. In 1832 two men were hanged at Ipswich for setting fire to the stables at the Crown. Years ago, the landlord gave his customers hot elderberry wine on the night before Cold Fair (9 or 21 December).

Minsmere. Note the motor cars. Edward Thomas stopped in a coastguard cottage here in 1907.

St Peter's Church, Theberton. The church is reputed to have had associations with smuggling. Edward Fitzgerald (1809-83) spoke of 'reports of Hollands found under the Altar Cloth of Theberton Church.' John Harvey, Pond Hall, near Hadley, Farmer, was tried at the Old Bailey in 1747 that he 'together with a number of 80 persons ... in the parish of Sheverton [Theberton] there carrying firearms and offensive weapons in order to commit the clandestine running of certain uncustomed goods.'

Church Corner, Theberton, in the early 1900s. The men from the raiding Zeppelin which was brought down here in the First World War were buried in the churchyard.

The Round House, Nuttery Lane, Theberton, 1908. Charles Montague Doughty, author of *Arabia Deserta*, was born at the Hall in 1843.

Sizewell, *c.* 1908. Sizewell Beach was of considerable significance during the eighteenth century when smuggling was rife and the Suffolk coast provided ideal natural facilities for the free traders.

The Coast Guard Station, Sizewell, 1906. In February 1775, Dragoons took six carts loaded with spirits at Sizewell; in March they captured fifteen carts, forty horses and six hundred tubs of spirits (about 2,400 gallons), as well as tea and dry goods.

HIGH ST., & POST OFFICE, LEISTON.

WHALES
PHOTOGRAPHIC

*Above:* Railway Station, Leiston, opened in 1859 and closed in 1966.

*Right:* Leiston Abbey Ruins, 1920.

*Opposite above:* High Street and Post Office, Leiston, 1906.

*Opposite below:* Blackhouse Corner, Leiston, in the 1930s.

Old Leiston, 1900. The houses which stood in Crown Street were demolished in the 1950s. In 1843, Leiston was only a large village with a population less than 1,200. By 1901 it had increased to over 3,000 (both figures include the population of Sizewell).

Snape Road, Leiston, in the early 1900s. The house in the centre was demolished and the site was occupied by Garretts Works.

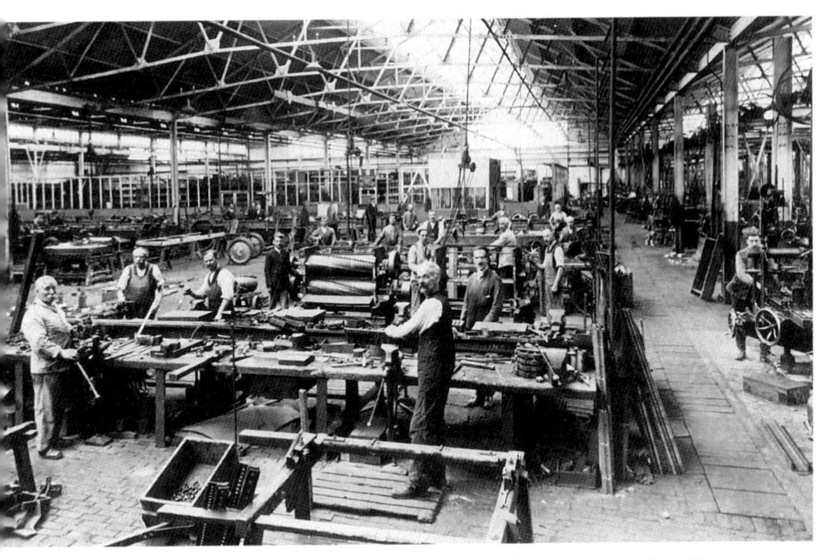

The fitting shop at Garretts, 1930s. Leiston was the home of the extensive and world-renowned Richard Garrett Works, established in 1778. The firm were specialists in agricultural machinery and had a large export market which came to include transport vehicles.

Sizewell Gap, *c.* 1900. On the left is Gap House. The area in the centre of the picture is now the site of a power station. Sizewell Gap, in Leiston parish and about two miles east of Leiston, used to have a Coastguard Station with rocket-saving apparatus, and also a fishery. Sizewell Gap was a favourite spot for smugglers. Now it is part of the Heritage Coast although, despite many protests, yet another nuclear power station is being erected.

Snape Races. Between 1727 and 1842, Snape was the site of an annual Race Meeting. The races were run over seven miles and 'much frequented by the London Jockies'. 'This is to inform all Persons, that on the tenth instant was a Match run on Snape Race Ground, between Mr William Spaulding of Rendham, and Mr Thomas Sympson, Drover, for Five Guineas. Mr Jack Spaulding Rare Jack against Mr Sympson Smiling Molley, the Six Rounds, which is according to Computation 7 miles in Sixteen Minuts; Mr Spaulding's Horse won the Match by Half a Horse's Nick, notwithstanding the Odds was a Guinea to Six-pence. N.B. Mr Spaulding's Horse run a 30 Miles Chase at Stag Hunting two Days after the said Race, and had 20 Miles Home to his Stable. O! RARE JACK!'

*Three*

# Aldringham, Thorpeness, Friston, Knodishall, Snape

'The delicate music of the Suffolk coast ... '
*Kenneth Clark*

Aldringham Parrot and Punchbowl (sixteenth century), c. 1912. Mr C.R. Wright, the Friston Miller, is standing with his horse and miller's cart with flour. Mr Frank Wolfe, standing in the doorway, was the publican. The picture shows several other Aldringham inhabitants both old and young, including girls with perambulator with occupant. On the right is the Aldringham Post Office.

Children on the Heath at Aldringham, *c.* 1912. The soil is a light sand and about 250 acres formed an open common.

Aldringham Post Office. Cecil Lay (1887-1956), the poet, artist and architect, was born at Aldringham and spent most of his life there.

Aldringham Chapel. A Baptist chapel built in 1812 and rebuilt in 1915. Note the burial ground adjoining the chapel.

A fatal aeroplane collision at Aldringham, 24 May 1910.

The Haven Bridge, Thorpe, on the Aldeburgh to Thorpeness road. The bridge was demolished c. 1932.

The beach, Thorpeness.

Thorpeness, 'this peculiar coastal settlement ... Much of it is half-timbered in a style which can only be classified as Stockbroker's Clerk's Tudor. It is all the brainchild of G. Stuart Ogilvie ... The utter absurdity of Thorpeness is not merely harmless but enjoyable.' (John Burke)

Friston Church.

Friston Street, 1912. Gadds Grocery and Cash Stores, the first shop in the district to sell ice cream – see the notice beneath the left window. A monkey in a cage used to be on the counter. Mr and Mrs Gadd are in front of the shop. The man with the gun under his arm is Mr Ward, the gamekeeper.

Travis and Forge, Friston. Standing by the travis, Mrs Bert Smith (the travis is where horses stood to be shod).

Knodishall Village, *c.* 1939. On the left, Fred Moore's Garage, opposite is Mrs Moore's General Shop. The white building in the centre is Fred Archer's Bicycle Shop.

Knodishall Mission Room and common, *c.* 1912. A horse fair used to be held on Cold Fair Green.

Grove Road, Friston, 1906. Around the 1830s Mr Hearn, a local shopkeeper, was working to create 'A Suffolk metropolism for Chartism.' Chartism and the Working Men's Association's first rally at Friston drew 1,000 people.

Friston Street, 1925, with the Chequers Inn on the left and on the right, the post mill which was working until 1955. The Friston Working Men's Association used to meet at the Chequers.

Snape Windmill, 1907. This post mill survived until 1933.

Sugar beet at Snape, when sugar beet was a strange crop in Suffolk. This sugar beet was grown with Dutch backing and being sent to Holland. A sugar beet factory was opened in Lavenham in 1869 and closed four years later because the farmers would not grow sugar beet. The crop did not become popular until it was subsidised in 1925.

Snape Village.

Thorpeness Halt, c. 1960. On the right, the goods station; in the centre, the passenger station. The Halt was closed by the Beeching Axe.

*Four*

# Aldeburgh

'A beautiful little sea town.'
*Thomas Carlyle*

The High Street, Aldburgh. The Old Custom House is the fourth house on the left, with steps. Aldeburgh was once a port, which, like a great part of the town, has been claimed by the sea.

The High Street.

The High Street. The poet George Crabbe was born at Slaughden, Aldeburgh, in 1754.

Spratting, Aldeburgh Beach, 1920-30. On the left is Curly Smith; standing in the boat is Charlie Mann. During the Second World War the sprat season dropped away and never recovered.

Fishermen on Aldeburgh Beach, late 1920s. On the left is Shakles Thorpe, ex-Royal navy, who had formerly served under Beatty. On the right is R. Thorpe.

The Hazard. A farmhouse just north of the river wall, destroyed by the sea in 1952.

Oakley Square pictured before 1925 when the Catholic church was built. Note the errand boy on the left, carrying a Hill and Reading hat box. The Post Office was blown up by a bomb on 4 December 1942.

Hill and Reading, Grocers and Provision Merchants, 1910. Standing in the doorway is Thomas Moyes. The shop's display of Zebra grate polish, Reckitts Blue and candles is typical of a shop-window of that time.

The Moot Hall *c.* 1900. The building dates back to the sixteenth century, but the twin Jacobean-style chimneys were added in 1854. It is now the Aldeburgh Museum and the Aldeburgh Council Chambers.

*Above:* A bathing machine on Aldeburgh Beach, 1920. In May 1793, James Neeves of the White Lion announced, 'Bathing machines are now ready, with careful guides to attend.'

*Left:* Aldeburgh Railway Station, 1919, with Ward's bus waiting to meet the train.

Aldeburgh Beach. In the 1860s there was a plan to build a pier, and building actually started near the Moot Hall in 1876. Unfortunately a barge did considerable damage to the spans already erected and the pier project was eventually abandoned. In 1851, all the lifeboats belonging to the Suffolk Association were taken under the control of the Royal National Lifeboat Institution and the Sizewell Lifeboat was moved to Aldeburgh and a boathouse was built on Slaughden Quay. Samuel Ward was appointed Coxwain. Later, the RNLI had a new lifeboat built for Aldeburgh which arrived in 1853. This boat, which was in service until 1870, was launched at least ten times, saving at least thirty-five lives. It was not named *Pasco* until 1866.

Lifeboat *The Aldeburgh* (1890-99), 1895. Built by J.H. Critten at a charge of £340 and powered by fourteen oars. This lifeboat had already been launched fifty-four times and saved one hundred and fifty-two lives when launched into a raging sea on 7 December 1899. The sea struck her on her broadside; the boat did not sink but was driven, keel uppermost, towards the shore. Five men were trapped under the boat and were drowned before a hole could be hacked in the side of the boat.

Lifeboat *City of Winchester* (1902-28), in 1924. *City of Winchester*, built by the Thomas Ironworks, was launched forty-three times and saved forty lives. James Cable was the coxswain of this lifeboat 1902-1917. He retired in 1917 after fifty years' service, nearly thirty as coxswain.

The Beach, Aldeburgh, 1905. Formerly bathing machines were drawn out of the water by a horse accompanied by a driver. By the 1890s, the horse and driver had gone. The machines then stood in rows, at first just above the high-water line and then, at a later date, at the top of the beach. Eventually, beach huts took their place.

Crag Path, Aldeburgh, c. 1902.

Fort Cottage, Crag path, *c.* 1898. Crag path – from Coralline Crag. The path is said to have been made by the navvies after they had completed the railway.

The Beach, Aldeburgh, *c.* 1900.

Crag Path, *c.* 1908. The tall building on the right is one of the two look-out towers. The towers belonged to the two rival beach companies, the Up-Towners and the Down-Towners, who offered help to vessels in distress. The rival companies competed for the spoils and salvage until the Royal National Lifeboat Institution put an end to the salvage gangs. One of the look-out towers is still used by the RNLI.

The Beach, *c.* 1909. 'I am happiest going in my little boat round the coast to Aldboro'.' (Edward Fitzgerald).

3, WENTWORTH TERRACE, ALDEBURGH.

The Town Steps in the early 1900s.

*Opposite above*: Wentworth Terrace, *c.* 1930. The Wentworth Hotel (on the right), was opened just before 1900. 'The hotel's frontage of 300 feet faced the German Ocean, and commanded an uninterrupted view of long expanse ... right up to the village of Thorpe.'

*Opposite below*: The Promenade in 1900. This was formerly a rough path used by fishermen for moving their catches. Note that both look-out towers can be seen in this photograph, although our attention is drawn towards the little girls and the perambulator.

High Street, *c.* 1900

High Street, *c.* 1900

High Street, *c.* 1905

High Street, *c.* 1910

HIGH STREET, ALDEBURGH
40909

Great Eastern Railway Station, early 1900s. Note the lamp posts, the women and the horse-drawn carriage by the entrance. The railway to Aldeburgh was an extension of the Saxmundham to Leiston branch line. Services began on 12 April 1860. It was then part of the East Suffolk Railway. The railway was a great advantage to the town, especially for the fishing industry. Seventy tons of sprats and other fish were sometimes dispatched by rail in one day. In 1862, the East Suffolk line and its branches were taken over by the Great Eastern Railway. During the Second World War armoured trains toured the line, carrying tank guns from the First World War. The passenger service closed on 12 September 1966.

*Opposite above:* High Street, *c.* 1905

*Opposite below:* Ward's Garage, with Standard and Austin motor cars.

The East Suffolk Hotel, High Street, in the early 1900s. In December 1903, the Aldeburgh Sprat Dinner was inaugurated at the East Suffolk Hotel. This hotel was originally called the Commercial Inn. In July 1668, after landing in Aldeburgh Bay, Charles II rested at this inn. The East Suffolk ran a horse bus to the station. Cobbolds fine ales were brewed at the Cliff Brewery, Ipswich. Charles Andrew Ward, a jobmaster, rented premises in the East Suffolk yard (right) and had a variety of horse-drawn vehicles for hire. Later, Charles Andrew Ward took over the hotel. At one time all but one member of the lifeboat crew was a Ward.

Victoria Road looking at Wentworth Road on the right and High Street on the left, early 1900s. The Cross Hotel is on the left, Woodcock and Henry, auctioneers, on the right. At the back on the left is The Moot Hall, with the Mill Inn in front of it. Note the woman on the left of the photograph, being pushed in a bath chair, and on the right, Mutticks handcart, the horse-drawn vehicle by the Mill Inn. The Cross provided stabling and Flintham, Hall & Co. Ltd's ales. This beer was brewed at the Albert Brewery in Station Road, Aldeburgh. The Brewery had five licensed houses in Aldeburgh when Adnams of Southwold took it over in 1924. Brewing then ceased at the Albert Brewery, which was later demolished.

Station Road Post Office.

The house boat, *Ionia*, which eventually burnt down.

Parade and beach.

Slaughden Quay, Aldeburgh's riverside. The seashore has been eaten away by the sea for centuries. Whole streets of houses have been devoured. George Crabbe, the poet, was born at Slaughden, the son of the saltmaster. In 1779, the house in which he was born was washed away. A Martello Tower, one of the eighteen built around Suffolk's coast, still stands. This is England's most northerly Martello Tower.

Slaughden Ferry. Three or four hundred years ago ships were built at this port.

Slaughden Ferry and the Three Mariners Inn. The warehouse, the cottages, and the inn have now been washed away by the sea.

The Three Mariners Inn, c. 1908. The inn held the ferry rights and was probably engaged in more smuggling than any other inn in Aldeburgh. When fishing smacks returned the sharing of profits took place in the inn. One of these smacks brought the whale's shoulder blade from Iceland – which is above the doorway and can now be seen in Aldeburgh Museum. The inn was swept away soon after this photograph was taken.

Mill House, originally a tower windmill, converted to a house in 1912 by the Revd W. Black.

Aldeburgh seen from Slaughden. The house boat, *Ionia*, can be seen in the background.

*Five*

# Orford, Hollesley, Alderton, Bawdsey

'Orford is a large, pleasant, waterside village of attractive corners.'
*Leonard P. Thompson*

Market Place, Orford, *c.* 1914. The town was granted a charter in 1579. It had a Mayor until 1886 and two Members of Parliament until 1852.

*Right*: Orford Lighthouse, 1906. This lighthouse was built in 1792. In the seventeenth century, Orford's first lighthouse was built of wood, with a coal fire for a beacon. It burnt down.

*Below*: The keep of Orford Castle, which is all that remains of a castle built during the twelfth century. On the left is the Crown and Castle Hotel which was built in 1879 on the site of an earlier inn.

*Opposite above*: Orford Church, which was rebuilt in the fourteenth century beside the ruins of the original church.

*Opposite below*: The ruins of Orford's original church.

The interior of Orford Castle from a photograph taken pre-1914.

Hollesley. Five Martello Towers were built at Hollesley Bay. By the middle of the nineteenth century all of them were occupied by coastguards.

Hollesley, 1906. Brendan Behan, the playwright, came here in 1939 to the Hollesley Bay penal establishment.

smallholder's cottage at the Hollesley Bay Training College. In the first experiment, 1887, the olonial College at Hollesley was intended to give training to people who had decided to emigrate. venty years later the second experiment was aiding the growing unemployment in London. Some milies settled in cottages on the estate although 'the provision of cottages and the development smallholdings was not contemplated by the Unemployed Workmen's Act.' Once the Colony had en deprived of its primary idea of providing 'permanent benefit' it became little better than a orified country workhouse, and the abandonment of this idea really meant the end of the second ollesley experiment.

The School, Alderton, *c.* 1913.

Alderton Congregational Church and Manse. S.W. Kitchiner, pastor.

T.W. Betts, Fish Merchant, Alderton.

Bawdsey Street *c.* 1920.

Bawdsey *c.* 1930

The Felixstowe-Bawdsey ferry across the Deben. A steam chain ferry was installed in 1894 and ceased working in 1931.

*Six*

# Felixstowe

'Felixstowe basks in the sunshine of fashion.'
*London Daily Chronicle, August 1906.*

The beach at Felixstowe seen from the pier. Walton (a manor before Felixstowe) merged with Felixstowe in an urban district council in 1895. In 1901 the combined population was 5,815; seven years later it had grown to 8,200.

Ferryman's House, Felixstowe. Felixstowe ferry had a Martello Tower, two inns, and a boatbuilders' yard. There are records of a ferry house dating back to 1181. Edward Fitzgerald was a frequent visitor at the Ferry Boat Inn and in 1863 he wrote, 'an inn with scarce table and chair and only bread and cheese to eat.'

Old Felixstowe. B.A. Steward, the agricultural journalist and author, spent his last years in Old Felixstowe.

Old Felixstowe Church, dating from the fourteenth century.

Hamilton Road, 1905. The main shopping street, named after the Duke of Hamilton, who was Lord of the Manor of Walton-cum-Trimley, of which Felixstowe was a part.

The beach shelter and restaurant, *c.* 1904, which had been erected by the District Council in 1899 at a cost of £2,759.

The Bath Hotel, 1914. The Suffragettes set fire to the Bath Hotel at 4.00am on 28 April 1914. It was entirely burnt out apart from the walls as can be seen from this front view of the hotel. The lodge of the convalescent home was later built on this site near the beach. The Bath Hotel, formerly the Hamilton Arms, was built with bricks from a Martello Tower which stood close by.

The Felix Hotel pre-1914. The original intention was to call this hotel the Balmoral. The building was finished in 1903, situated on the cliff in twelve acres of grounds, its terraces extending to the beach. It had one hundred and sixty-nine letting rooms, fifty-two bathrooms, four lounges and a dining room to seat four hundred and fifty people.

A fine array of motor cars outside the Felix Hotel in the early 1900s. The Felix had a garage for fi
cars as well as twenty-one tennis courts and two croquet lawns.

Felixstowe Beach Station. Felixstowe had three railway stations. Both the Beach and the Pier stations were opened on 1 May 1877. The Town station was not erected until 1898. In 1879 the li was acquired by the Great Eastern Railway.

Off for a ride. Donkeys were popular in Felixstowe by the middle of the nineteenth century. An old man who was very deaf, Mr Rattle, was in charge of five donkeys and two carts in 1854.

Naval seaplanes at Felixstowe, *c.* 1916. A station for the development of seaplanes was established at Felixstowe in 1913. The station remained open until the late 1950s.

46990. FELIXSTOWE: CONVALESCENT HILL.

The Promenade, with the convalescent home on the right. Felixstowe had begun to have a reputation as a holiday resort by the middle of the nineteenth century and it is largely this aspect which features in the photographs in this selection. Its development as a resort was increased by the publicity given to the visit of the German Empress and her children in 1891. The presence of the railway brought holidaymakers to the town. But twentieth-century Felixstowe has almost hidden the ancient town where Edward III had a residence.

*Opposite above*: Barlet Convalescent Home, built in 1923 on the site of a former Martello Tower.

*Opposite below*: Convalescent Hill.

The promenade, *c.* 1910. The sea front and promenade were constructed *c.* 1902 by the Felixstowe and Walton Urban District Council at a cost of £36,000.

The bathing machine was introduced by Benjamin Beale, a Margate Quaker, in the 1750s. Mixed bathing was anathema in Victorian days but in the early 1900s it was permitted at all times at Felixstowe. These bathing machines appear to be advertising pills on their sides.

Butlins Amusement Park, 1930s.

Butlins Amusement Park, 1930s.

The beach, *c.* 1909. Felixstowe boasted that it had more ozone than any other place, and was considered 'one of the most improving places on the east coast' because 'many leading inhabitants of the district have their residence there.'

Cobbold's Point, *c.* 1909.

The Spa Pavilion, *c.* 1910, formerly the Flora Hall, bombed in 1941. The author George Meredith was a visitor to Felixstowe; Alan Jobson, author of numerous books on Suffolk also lived there, and so did the novelist Robert Greenwood.

Promenade and Model Yacht Pool, 1930s. Felixstowe is the only town on the Suffolk coast with a southern aspect.

Bathing machines in the early 1900s. Unlike most seaside resorts, horses were not used to draw the bathing machines out of the water. Instead, they were drawn out by means of a winch. Some winches and ropes can be seen in this picture.

Cobbold's Point *c.* 1906. The Promenade, starting at Cobbold's Point, was two miles in length. When J.C. Cobbold, MP and Ipswich magnate, built a mansion at what was then The Point it became known as Cobbold's Point. J.C. Cobbold built the Bath Hotel in 1839. In the mid-nineteenth century there were already a number of beach huts here but only three bathing machines.

The Bay and the Pier, 1937. A new pier was built in 1904 by the Coast Development Company. It was half a mile long until reduced to a stump after the Second World War. The Belle Steamers, which ran between Yarmouth and London, called at the end of the pier. The Great Eastern Railway Company's river steamers sailed daily between Felixstowe, Ipswich, and Harwich.

The pier entrance in the 1930s. The pier had an electric tram as well as shelters.

From the pier, looking east, 1907. Note the groynes and breakwaters in the bay.

Paddling, *c.* 1935. When bathing first became popular, in the early eighteenth century, mixed bathing was the normal procedure and neither sex deemed it necessary to wear anything.

From this photograph it almost seems that the sexes were not allowed to mix even on the beach.

W.A. Squires, Family Butcher, 249 High Street, Walton.

Walton High Street, Salvation Army Barracks, 1908.

Walton, *c.* 1900. Walton was the nearest place around Felixstowe with shops in the mid-nineteenth century.

*Seven*

# People and Occasions

'They have seen what we shall never see. They have heard the sound of silence.'

*Michael Watkins*

An Aldeburgh occasion. The Moot Hall at the back, the Mill Inn on the left, and bathing machines on the shore. The occasion is the Flower Show and the Parade is about to start.

*Above*: Another Aldeburgh Parade, the Easter Sunday Mayoral Procession, *c.* 1910.

*Opposite above*: A picnic outing from the Belgian Children's Home, Aldeburgh, 1916. During the First World War there were many Belgian refugees in England.

Thomas Hardy (right) with Edward Clodd on the beach at Aldeburgh, *c.* 1910. Other famous literary men who were fond of Aldeburgh include Edward Fitzgerald, Wilkie Collins, Thomas Carlyle, George Meredith and E.M. Forster – although Forster called it 'A bleak little place, not beautiful.' Edward Clodd, founder of the Omar Khayam Club, lived at Stratford House in Aldeburgh, where Hardy stayed.

Aldeburgh Cricket Team, Kings Field, 1907.

Men of Aldeburgh: Tom Parnell, Hector Burrell, Shuggy Goldsmith, Victor Fisher, Johnny Burrell.

Walberswick Cinema, shortly before it closed in 1950. It opened as a private cinema and then opened for troops stationed at Walberswick during the Second World War. There was room for six people in the balcony. Note the photographs of film stars.

Friston men pre-1939: Archie Howard, carpenter; Wally Smith, bricklayer; Gus Ransby, the guv'nor and carpenter; Arthur Butcher, general handiman.

Station Mill, Aldeburgh.

Ploughing with Suffolk Punches, near Aldeburgh. Setting-up of the top at the start of ploughing. The man's clothes suggest that this was a ploughing match.

A pause during mowing near Aldeburgh.

At Friston Mill when it was still working, Bernard Cook, Billy Lowe and George Coxage during the 1950s. This photograph was taken by Bob Wright, who worked in the mill.

Friston Steel Quoits Team, 1913.

The Smith Family of Friston. The Smiths were blacksmiths

Annie Marsley (later Mrs Alan Ralph), c. 1910. She became a Sunday School teacher at Friston Baptist Chapel.

Will Moss, thatcher of Friston, known as 'Cock Eye.' (early 1930s).

Hector Burrell, mending nets on Aldeburgh beach.

Scout Jamboree at Knodishall on 25 August 1917.

The Knodishall Coronation Festivities Committee, coronation of King George V.

Friston Bowls Club, c. 1936.

*Above*: The Shepherd's House (just south of the Martello Tower at Slaughden). Mr Winter and his family. Dan Winter looked after the stock on the marshes at Slaughden. The house was later lost to the sea.

*Left*: Aldeburgh Railway Signal Box, 1920s, with Messrs Fryer, Bottrell and Knights.

*Opposite*: Dan Wilson of Aldeburgh, fisherman, lifeboatman, and a survivor of the Aldeburgh Lifeboat Disaster of 7 December 1899 when six members of the crew were killed by drowning and a seventh who died of his injuries the following March. Mr Wilson was also starter for the Aldeburgh Yacht Club.

ALDEBURGH LIFEBOAT

Men of Westleton, *c.* 1900.

Wheelwrights at Hollesley, *c.* 1900.

The menu for the Sprat Dinner held on 1 January 1908 was:

Sprats – Boiled, Fried, Savoury
Old English Fare – The Roast Beef of Old England
Plumb Pudding, Mince Pies
Cheese and Celery

One of the toasts was to 'The Spratting Industry.' The annual dinners lasted from 1903 to 1913. At the one held in January 1912 it was stated that the catches had been much below those of previous years. There were then ninety spratters and twenty-four boats.

Will C. Pepper's White Coons, Felixstowe, 1906: Mr Percy Watson, Mr Alf Wood, Miss Gladys Clare, Mr Ben Lawes, and Mr Stanley Kirby (with a London office at 97a Jermyn Street).

Pierrots at Felixstowe, *c.* 1910. 'The first three rows of chairs 2d each. Others 1d.' Black minstrels arrived from America in the mid-nineteenth century to vanish fifty years later and be replaced by pierrots.

Aldeburgh Town Band, *c.* 1910.

Workmen at Leiston, *c.* 1910.

Friston School, the Middle Classes, *c.* 1934.

The Mill Laundry at Aldeburgh with Miss Pettit with her staff, *c.* 1900. Apparently Miss Pettit also ran a 'Registry Office for Servants.'

Fred Norman's Foundry at Knodishall in the 1930s. The Foundry was casting brass and iron until *c.* 1934. Fred Norman is in the centre.

F. Norman & Son, Blacksmith, Knodishall, *c.* 1937. General blacksmiths, here they are 'shoeing a wagon'– a hot iron tyre has been put on a wheel, they are now cooling it with water and the tyre will contract and fit tightly to the felloes of the wooden wheel. Wheelwrights made wagons and carts as well as wheels but blacksmiths often fitted the tyres. Pictured are Mr Bradnum, Fred Wollnough and Robert Norman.

Men of Walberswick: Albert English, Tow Cooper, Wesy Cross, and George English.

Aldeburgh People c. 1910. First from left is Wacky Downing, Simon Fisher is next to him. The building behind them is now the British Legion Hall.

Old age pensioners at Darsham in January 1908, during the first week pensions were issued. The first pensions were only for persons over seventy years of age who had been British subjects for at least twenty years. Their pension was five shillings (25p) per week.

Bulcamp Workhouse (Blythburgh Union) in the 1880s, with men and boy inmates. The master and his wife and the chaplain (with the white coat and long beard) are standing on the left. On the right are two members of the Southwold Volunteers and the schoolmaster. This workhouse was opened in 1766.

An emergency landing at Snape in 1913.

The Lifeboat *Edward Z. Dresden*, 1906, launched at Slaughden when, it was reported, 'the noise was awful.' It was in service at No. 2 Station, Aldeburgh, 1905-1929. Fifty-six launches were made and forty-two lives were saved.

This photograph was taken outside The Gables at the bottom of Lee Road, Aldeburgh.

# Picture Credits

The photographs are from the collections of:

Aldeburgh Museum, Philip Kett, David Moyse, Derrick Neave, Humphrey Phelps, Jack Smith, John Tooke, and Bob Wright.

Felixstowe Town Station, c. 1900.